Treasures of The Vatican Library
(Book Illustration, Volume 6)

For It Is Written...

Turner Publishing, Inc.

ATLANTA

The illustrations in this book are taken from Latin manuscript volumes in the collections of
The Vatican Library, including the Barberini, Chigi, Reginense, and Urbino collections.
The sources for each illustration appear on page 80.

Published by Turner Publishing, Inc.
A Subsidiary of Turner Broadcasting System, Inc.
1050 Techwood Drive, N.W.
Atlanta, Georgia 30318

First Edition 10 9 8 7 6 5 4 3 2 1

Library of Congress Cataloging-in-Publication Data
For it is Written. . . —1st ed.
p. cm. —(Treasures of the Vatican Library)
Contains illustrations from various Vatican Library manuscripts with each illustration
accompanied by a Bible scripture from the New Revised Standard Version Bible.
ISBN 1-57036-232-7 (alk. paper)
1. Initials. 2. Illumination of books and manuscripts, Medieval.
3. Illumination of books and manuscripts—Vatican City. 4. Biblioteca apostolica vaticana.
I. Biblioteca apostolica vaticana. II. Turner Publishing, Inc.
III. Bible. English. New Revised Standard. Selections. 1995. IV. Series.
ND3335.F67   1995
745.6'7'0940902—dc20   95-170
CIP

Printed in Hong Kong.

For It Is Written...

ESIDRII MEIDESI

Treasures of The Vatican Library:
Book Illustration

$\mathcal{F}$OR IT IS WRITTEN..., the sixth volume in the Treasures of The Vatican Library series, offers a selection of miniature masterworks of book illustration from the collections of one of the world's greatest repositories of classical, medieval, and Renaissance culture. The Vatican Library, for six hundred years celebrated as a center of learning and a monument to the art of the book, is, nevertheless, little known to the general public, for admission to the library traditionally has been restricted to qualified scholars. Since very few outside the scholarly community have ever been privileged to examine the magnificent hand-lettered and illuminated manuscript books in the library's collections, the artwork selected for the series volumes is all the more poignant, fascinating, and appealing.

Of course, the popes had always maintained a library, but in the fifteenth century, Pope Nicholas V decided to build an edifice of unrivaled magnificence to house the papacy's growing collections—to serve the entire "court of Rome," the clerics and scholars associated with the papal palace. Pope Sixtus IV added to what Nicholas had begun, providing the library with a suite of beautifully frescoed rooms and furnishing it with heavy wooden benches, to which the precious works were actually chained. But, most significantly, like the popes who succeeded him, Sixtus added books. By 1455 the library held 1,200 volumes, and a catalogue compiled in 1481 listed 3,500, making it by far the largest collection of books in the Western world.

And The Vatican Library has kept growing: through purchase, commission, donation, and military conquest. Nor did the popes restrict themselves to ecclesiastical subjects. Bibles, theological texts, and commentaries on canon law are here in abundance, to be sure, but so are the Latin and Greek classics that placed The Vatican Library at the very heart of all Renaissance learning. Over the centuries, the library has acquired some of the world's most significant collections of literary works, including the Palatine Library of Heidelberg, the Cerulli collection of Persian and Ethiopian manuscripts, the great Renaissance libraries of the Duke of Urbino and of Queen Christina of Sweden, and the matchless seventeenth-century collections of the Barberini, the Ottoboni, and Chigi. Today the library contains over one million printed books—including eight thousand published during the first fifty years of the printing press—in addition to 150,000 manuscripts and some 100,000 prints. Assiduously collected and carefully preserved over the course of almost six hundred years, these unique works of art and knowledge, ranging from the secular to the profane, are featured in this ongoing series, Treasures of The Vatican Library, for the delectation of lovers of great books and breathtaking works of art.

IN THE
BEGINNING
WAS THE WORD,
AND THE WORD
WAS WITH GOD,
AND THE WORD
WAS GOD.

JOHN 1:1

OF MAKING

MANY BOOKS

THERE IS NO

END, AND MUCH

STUDY IS A

WEARINESS OF

THE FLESH.

ECCLESIASTES 12:12

"AM I MY BROTHER'S KEEPER?"

GENESIS 4:9

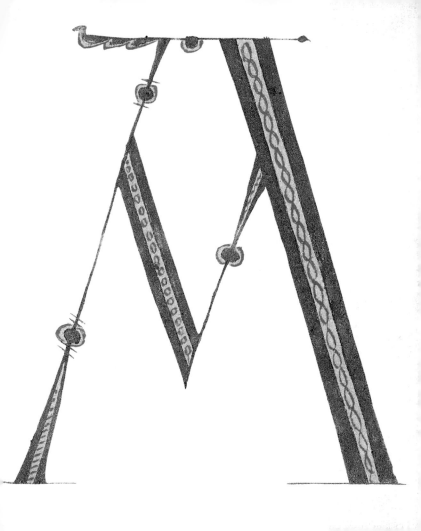

BETTER IS

THE END OF

A THING THAN

ITS BEGINNING.

ECCLESIASTES 7:8

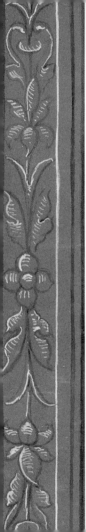

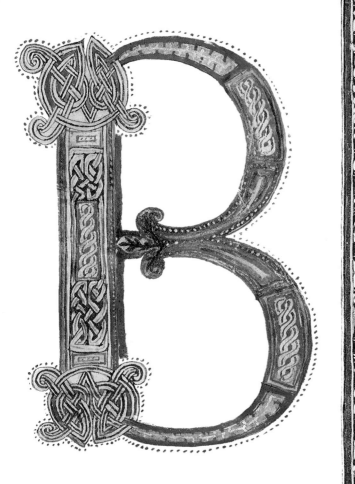

"COME
TO ME, ALL YOU
THAT ARE WEARY AND
ARE CARRYING HEAVY BURDENS,
AND I WILL GIVE YOU REST.
TAKE MY YOKE UPON YOU,
AND LEARN FROM ME; FOR I AM
GENTLE AND HUMBLE IN HEART,
AND YOU WILL FIND REST
FOR YOUR SOULS."

MATTHEW 11:28-29

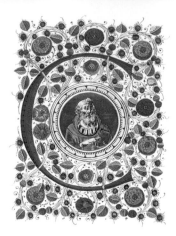

"DO NOT JUDGE, SO
THAT YOU MAY NOT BE
JUDGED. FOR WITH THE
JUDGMENT YOU MAKE YOU
WILL BE JUDGED, AND THE
MEASURE YOU GIVE WILL BE
THE MEASURE YOU GET."

MATTHEW 7:1–2

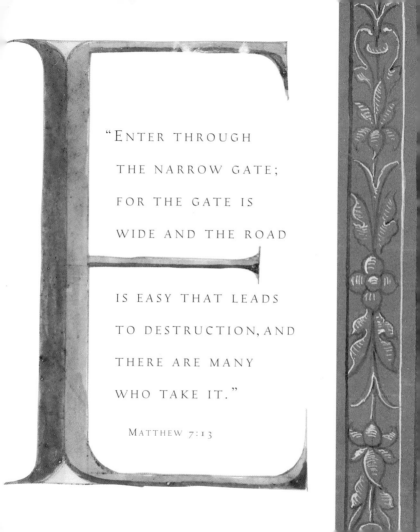

"ENTER THROUGH
THE NARROW GATE;
FOR THE GATE IS
WIDE AND THE ROAD

IS EASY THAT LEADS
TO DESTRUCTION, AND
THERE ARE MANY
WHO TAKE IT."

MATTHEW 7:13

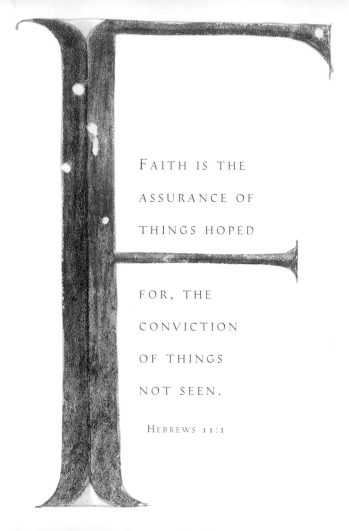

FAITH IS THE
ASSURANCE OF
THINGS HOPED

FOR, THE
CONVICTION
OF THINGS
NOT SEEN.

HEBREWS 11:1

GUARD ME AS
THE APPLE OF
THE EYE; HIDE ME
IN THE SHADOW
OF YOUR WINGS.

PSALM 17:8

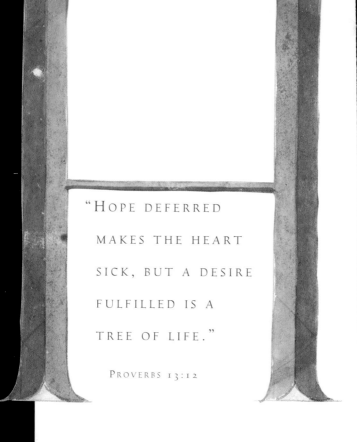

"HOPE DEFERRED
MAKES THE HEART
SICK, BUT A DESIRE
FULFILLED IS A
TREE OF LIFE."

PROVERBS 13:12

I WILL

LIFT UP

MINE EYES

TO THE

HILLS—

FROM

WHERE

WILL

MY HELP

COME?

PSALM 121:1

JUSTICE IS
TURNED BACK, AND
RIGHTEOUSNESS
STANDS AT A
DISTANCE; FOR
TRUTH STUMBLES IN
THE PUBLIC SQUARE,
AND UPRIGHTNESS
CANNOT ENTER.

ISAIAH 59:14

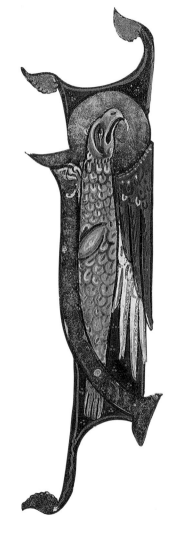

KNOWLEDGE

PUFFS UP,

BUT LOVE

BUILDS UP.

1 CORINTHIANS 8:1

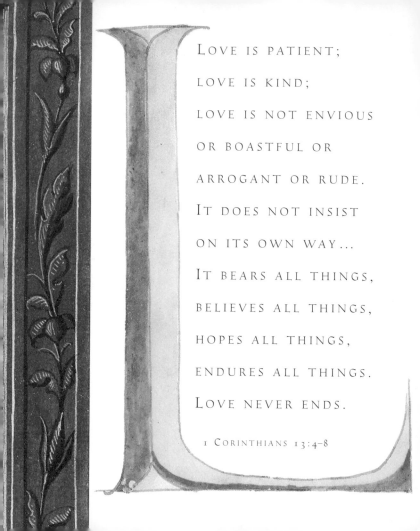

LOVE IS PATIENT;

LOVE IS KIND;

LOVE IS NOT ENVIOUS

OR BOASTFUL OR

ARROGANT OR RUDE.

IT DOES NOT INSIST

ON ITS OWN WAY...

IT BEARS ALL THINGS,

BELIEVES ALL THINGS,

HOPES ALL THINGS,

ENDURES ALL THINGS.

LOVE NEVER ENDS.

1 CORINTHIANS 13:4-8

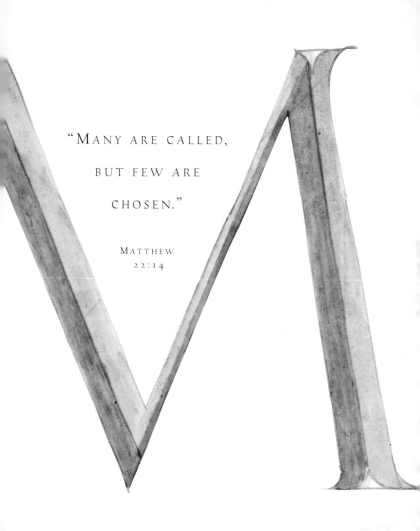

"MANY ARE CALLED,

BUT FEW ARE

CHOSEN."

MATTHEW
22:14

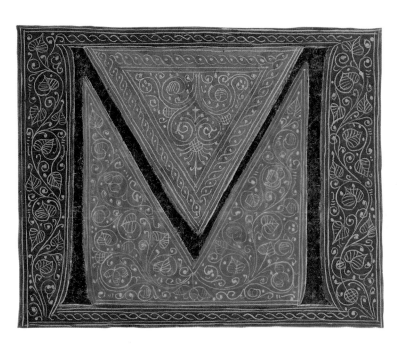

"No one has greater love than this, to lay down one's life for one's friends."

John 15:13

"O THAT MY WORDS
WERE WRITTEN DOWN!
O THAT THEY WERE INSCRIBED
IN A BOOK! O THAT WITH AN
IRON PEN AND WITH LEAD
THEY WERE ENGRAVED ON
A ROCK FOREVER!"

JOB 19:23-24

PUT NOT

YOUR TRUST

IN PRINCES...

PSALM 146:3

QUIET WORDS OF
THE WISE ARE MORE
TO BE HEEDED THAN
THE SHOUTING OF A
RULER AMONG FOOLS.

ECCLESIASTES 9:17

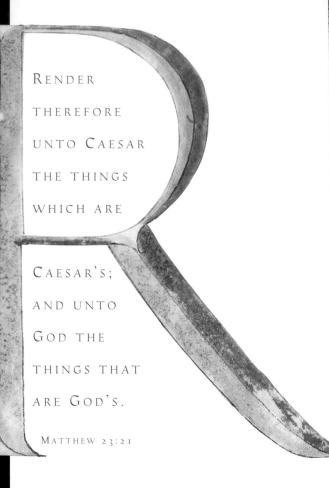

RENDER
THEREFORE
UNTO CAESAR
THE THINGS
WHICH ARE

CAESAR'S;
AND UNTO
GOD THE
THINGS THAT
ARE GOD'S.

MATTHEW 23:21

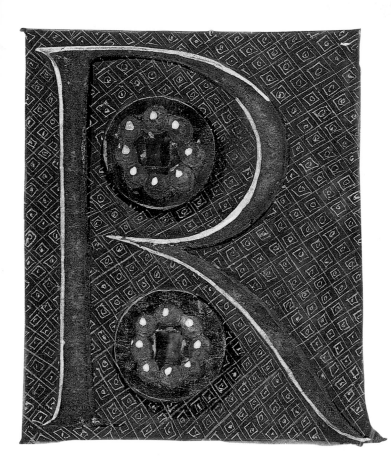

SEND OUT YOUR BREAD

UPON THE WATERS,

FOR AFTER MANY DAYS

YOU WILL GET IT BACK.

ECCLESIASTES 11:1

THE LETTER KILLS, BUT THE SPIRIT

GIVES

LIFE.

2 CORINTHIANS 3:6

UNTO

THE PURE

ALL THINGS

ARE PURE.

TITUS 1:15

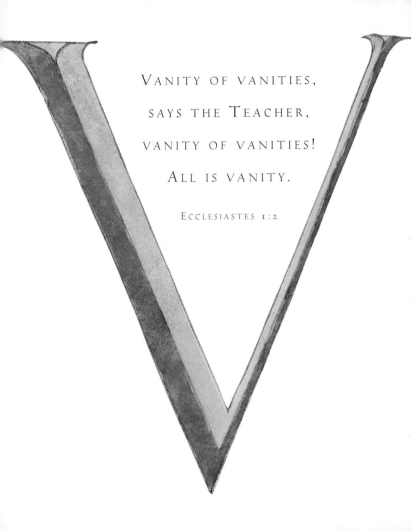

Vanity of vanities,
says the Teacher,
vanity of vanities!
All is vanity.

Ecclesiastes 1:2

WHAT ARE
HUMAN BEINGS
THAT YOU ARE
MINDFUL OF
THEM, MORTALS
THAT YOU CARE
FOR THEM?

PSALM 8:4

ILLUSTRATIONS

Cover and half-title page: Reg. Lat. 128 fol. 20 r; frontispiece: Urb. Lat. 1 fol. 4 v; p. 7: Urb. Lat. 450 fol. 216 r; p. 12: Vat. Lat. 6852 fol. 1 r; p.14: Reg. Lat. 226 fol. 52 r; p. 15: Reg. Lat. 245 fol. 1 r; p. 16 Reg. Lat. 339 fol. 41 r; p. 17: Urb. Lat. 405 fol. 1 r; p. 18: Vat. Lat. 6852 fol. 1 v; p. 19: Reg. Lat. 104 fol. 2 r; p. 20: Reg. Lat. 128 fol. 135 r, Urb. Lat. 392 fol. 2 r; p. 21: Reg. Lat. 482 fol. 1 v, Vat. Lat. 392 fol. 2 r; p. 22: Urb. Lat. 185 fol. 68 r; p. 23: Vat. Lat. 6852 fol. 2 r; p. 24: Urb. Lat. 319 fol. 2 r, Urb. Lat. 332 fol. 1 r; p. 26: Vat. Lat. 6852 fol. 2 v; p. 27: Vat. Lat. 711 fol. 63 r; p. 31: Vat. Lat. 6852 fol. 3 r; p. 32: Reg. Lat. 226 fol. 53 r; p. 33: Urb. Lat. 432 fol. 4 r; p. 34: Vat. Lat. 6852 fol. 3 v; p. 35: Urb. Lat. 1 fol. 37 r, Urb. Lat. 392 fol. 2 r; p. 36: Urb. Lat. 2 fol. 272 r; p. 37: Vat. Lat. 6852 fol. 4 r; p. 38: Vat. Lat. 6852 fol. 4 v; p. 39: Vat. Lat. 1269 fol. 23 r; p. 40: Urb. Lat. 192 fol. 1 r, Barb. Lat. 425 fol. 27 r; p. 41: Vat. Lat. 6852 fol. 5 r; p. 42: Reg. Lat. 119 fol. 2 r; 43: Reg. Lat. 6 fol. 3 r; p. 44: Vat. Lat. 6852 fol. 5 v; 46: Vat. Lat. 6852 fol. 6 r; p. 47: Urb. Lat. 1 fol. 39 r; p. 48: Urb. Lat. 373 fol. 1 r; p. 49: Vat. Lat. 6852 fol. 6 v; p. 50: Urb. Lat. 2 fol. 161 r; p. 52: Urb. Lat. 2 fol. 297 r; p. 53: Vat. Lat. 6852 fol. 7 r; p. 54: Vat. Lat. 6852 fol. 7 v; p. 55: Urb. Lat. 185 fol. 34 v; p. 56: Vat. Lat. 711 fol. 1 r, Barb. Lat. 610 fol. 256 r; p. 57: Urb. Lat. 450 fol. 216 r; p. 58: Reg. Lat. 691 fol. 1 r; p. 59: Urb. Lat. 406 fol. 2 r; p. 60: Urb. Lat. 185 fol. 60 r; p. 61: Vat. Lat. 6852 fol. 13 r, Vat. Lat. 392 fol. 2 r; p. 62: Vat. Lat. 6852 fol. 8 v; p. 63: Chigi C VIII 228 fol. 106 r; p. 64: Reg. Lat. 103 fol. 17 v; p. 65: Urb. Lat. 220 fol. 2 r; p. 66: Reg. Lat. 128 fol. 20 r; p. 67: Vat. Lat. 1787 fol. 8 v; p. 68: Reg. Lat. 34 fol. 34 v; p. 69: Vat. Lat. 555 fol. 41 r, Vat. Lat. 214 fol. 30 v; p. 70: Vat. Lat. 146 fol. 1 r, Urb. Lat. 207 fol. 2 r; p. 71: Vat. Lat. 6852 fol. 10 v; p. 72: Vat. Lat. 2194 fol. 5 v; p. 74: Vat. Lat. 1320 fol. 1 r, Urb. Lat. 1 fol. 12 v; p. 75: Vat. Lat. 6852 fol. 11 r; p. 76: Reg. Lat. 128 fol. 135 r; p. 77: Urb. Lat. 1 fol. 66 v; p. 78: Vat. Lat. 392 fol. 2 r, Vat. Lat. 6852 fol. 11 v; p. 79: Vat. Lat. 6952 fol. 12 r, Vat. Lat. 6852 fol. 12 v. Ornamental illumination on pp. 8 and 11 is from Urb. Lat. 207 fol. 2 r. Ornamental illumination on pp. 12 and 13 is from Urb. Lat. 308 fol. 2 r. Ornamental illumination on pp. 14, 29, 46, and 64 is from Reg. Lat. 128 fol. 53 v. Ornamental illumination on pp. 24 and 25 is from Urb. Lat. 441 fol. 2 r. Ornamental illumination on pp. 28 and 45 is from Urb. Lat. 403 fol. 1 r. Ornamental illumination on pp. 30 and 31 is from Reg. Lat. 128 fol. 135 r. Ornamental illumination on pp. 50 and 51 is from Urb. Lat. 128 fol. 9 r.